MAYBE TOMORROW

DRAMA

Kraftgriots

Also in the series (DRAMA)

Rasheed Gbadamosi: *Trees Grow in the Desert*
Rasheed Gbadamosi: *3 Plays*
Akomaye Oko: *The Cynic*
Chris Nwamuo: *The Squeeze & Other Plays*
Olu Obafemi: *Naira Has No Gender*
Chinyere Okafor: *Campus Palavar & Other Plays*
Chinyere Okafor: *The Lion and the Iroko*
Ahmed Yerima: *The Silent Gods*
Ebereonwu: *Cobweb Seduction*
Ahmed Yerima: *Kaffir's Last Game*
Ahmed Yerima: *The Bishop & the Soul* with *Thank You Lord*
Ahmed Yerima: *The Trials of Oba Ovonramwen*
Ahmed Yerima: *Attahiru*
Ahmed Yerima: *The Sick People* (2000)
Omome Anao: *Lions at War & Other Plays* (2000)
Ahmed Yerima: *Dry Leaves on Ukan Trees* (2001)
Ahmed Yerima: *The Sisters* (2001)
Niyi Osundare: *The State Visit* (2002)
Ahmed Yerima: *Yemoja* (2002)
Ahmed Yerima: *The Lottery Ticket* (2002)
Muritala Sule: *Wetie* (2003)
Ahmed Yerima: *Otaelo* (2003)
Ahmed Yerima: *The Angel & Other Plays* (2004)
Ahmed Yerima: *The Limam & Ade Ire* (2004)
Onyebuchi Nwosu: *Bleeding Scars* (2005)
Ahmed Yerima: *Ameh Oboni the Great* (2006)
Femi Osofisan: *Fiddlers on a Midnight Lark* (2006)
Ahmed Yerima: *Hard Ground* (2006), winner, The Nigeria Prize for Literature, 2006 and winner, ANA/NDDC J.P. Clark Drama Prize, 2006
Ahmed Yerima: *Idemili* (2006)
Ahmed Yerima: *Erelu-Kuti* (2006)
Austine E. Anigala: *Cold Wings of Darkness* (2006)
Austine E. Anigala: *The Living Dead* (2006)
Felix A. Akinsipe: *Never and Never* (2006)
Ahmed Yerima: *Aetu* (2007)
Chukwuma Anyanwu: *Boundless Love* (2007)
Ben Binebai: *Corpers' Verdict* (2007)
John Iwuh: *The Village Lamb* (2007), winner, ANA/NDDC J.P. Clark Drama Prize, 2008
Chris Anyokwu: *Ufuoma* (2007)
Ahmed Yerima: *The Wives* (2007)

MAYBE TOMORROW

DRAMA

Soji Cole

kraftgriots

Published by

Kraft Books Limited
6A Polytechnic Road, Sango, Ibadan
Box 22084, University of Ibadan Post Office
Ibadan, Oyo State, Nigeria
✆ 0803 348 2474, 0805 129 1191
E-mail: kraftbooks@yahoo.com

First published 2013

ISBN: 978-978-918-080-6

= KRAFTGRIOTS =
(A literary imprint of Kraft Books Limited)

First printing, October 2013

In Memoriam

This one
For her where
Troubles will reach her no more
Enjoying the phenomena of unassailable goods

Gbemisola Aduni Cole (IYA AWE)

Production Vitae

Maybe Tomorrow had an experimental run at the Arts Theatre, University of Ibadan between April 2 and 4, 2008 under the auspices of FOLK HERITAGE MULTIMEDIA COMPANY. The production team was made up of the following:

Cast

KO:	Simi Hassan
AW:	Andrew Adigwe (Shubby)
2 POLICEMEN:	Played in voice-over and light manipulation according to the director's experimental style.

Crew

Sound:	Ayo Atoki Gabriel Afolayan Bayo Ariyibi
Light:	Samson Akapo Anthony Ayodele
Publicity:	Tolu Fagbure Kola Adewale Debola Ogunshina Ben Ogunmodede Tunde Lawal
Management:	Jumoke Adelu Bidemi Ojeomokhai Mide Onikosi Joy Akunafiaru Bukola Majekodunmi

Box Office:	Bimbo Benson
Stage Manager:	Tunde Ojobaro
Asst. Director:	Bayo Ariyibi
Director:	Ayo Atoki

Characters

Kenule Ododo (KO):	A civil war veteran, now the leader of a Niger Delta militant group.
Adolphus Wariboko(AW):	Also a civil war veteran, now a Nigerian police officer.

2 POLICEMEN

Darkness: A police interrogation room where the suspect is to be cross-examined. Dim light gradually comes on stage, creating a tense feeling of abject solitude. At centre stage of the room are a table and a chair; empty. Also centre stage, a little to the left is a lone chair; also empty. On the walls are various posters with mantras peculiar to the Nigeria police: "Help police fight crime", "Police is your friend", "Bail is free", etc. Presently, a suspect is brought in by two policemen. He is pulled to the seat by the left. Light comes fully on stage. The interrogator walks in with face beaming with expressionless humility.

AW: (*To the policemen.*) You may leave. *(They leave.)* Kenule Ododo, I am sorry my boys ill-treated you. (*Silence.*) Kenule Ododo.

KO: I was sure you're the one they would send to me.

AW: I hope this discussion will be without animus. (*Silence. He reads from a paper.*) "Mr Kenule Ododo, leader, Coastal Fighters Group, led five violent demonstrations within five years ..."

KO: (*Snapping.*) Those demonstrations were not meant to be violent!

AW: But they were! They were, my friend! Kenule, I want this discussion to be as amiable as possible and I guess that was why they sent me in to interrogate you; if for nothing else but old ties — friendship. Don't make things difficult for the two of us; and remember that the civil war taught us impatience, so don't stir it! I suggest that you open up to me so that I can help you as best as I can.

(*Silence.*) I am sorry. I didn't intend to shout at you, but you see, the language of communication is not easy, especially from a policeman to a suspect. I know that you are sensitive enough to know the line that divides friendship and duty.

KO: (*With lukewarm resentment.*) Yes, I know. That was why we both chose different ways after the war to serve our nation.

AW: But you should know that the way you have chosen breeds violence.

KO: No. It rather amplifies the voice of the people.

AW: It does? I hope so and I do sympathize with your cause. But I must tell you that some things are better left for God to judge.

KO: (*Stands.*) You are mistaken. You think God sits and watches his people beaten and plundered? No! In his silence he speaks to us: "Go, my children, fight your battle yourselves!"

AW: You're becoming prophetic. But you learn in the Bible that if you're slapped on the right cheek you turn the left also to be slapped?

KO: (*Chuckles.*) We the people of the coast are not that foolish! You give us a slap on the right cheek, we will return it with three violent slaps. That portion of the Bible was never meant for us.

AW: (*Assuming an unhurried manner of speaking.*) Well, we must start the business that brought us here. I take it that a word may not be enough for the wise.

This is why I am taking my time to speak to you in this manner. Things need to be explained to the wise. Only the foolish these days get satisfied with a word. (*Suddenly acting formal.*) Mr Kenule Ododo, leader, Coastal Fighters Group, I ask you in the name of the law, where are you hiding the two expatriates your group kidnapped?

KO: (*Defiantly.*) I am bored with the same question for the past seventy-two hours!

AW: (*Loses his calm.*) Where are you keeping them?

KO: I don't know what you are talking about! It's a surprise that the police have taught you a different kind of impatience. No decorum; even to friends.

AW: I warned you earlier that a line cuts friendship from duty. (*Prolonged silence.*) You are not speaking?

KO: (*looking distant.*) I am.

AW: (*Confused.*) You are not.

KO: There is speaking in silence. The silence of the common man is full of words. It is full of speeches that will not be heard even if they are uttered. Adolphus ... you have changed. Were you not the same soldier who carried me on your back, trudging with painful strides for nearly two kilometres when I was shot at Abagana during the war? In my faint consciousness I saw tears sliding down your cheeks and heard your heart echoing that you would risk every bullet to get me to the camp.

AW: Yesterday is a memory.

KO: Are you not the same soldier who shared my idea of a better country if the corrupt and tyrannical government was overthrown?

AW: I have not changed my mind.

KO: Yes, you have not! But your memory cannot be so clouded to forget our discovery years after the war: the government whom we had sided to turn the guns against our own people had no place for us!

AW: That was old times. Things have changed; the new government is trying.

KO: There is nothing new about the government. It is old wine in a new bottle. They carry the regimented values of the old politicians.

AW: Our anger will do nothing to move the country forward. We must support the government.

KO: Yes we must, but first, I must support my people. Call it tribalism if you want, but I must tell you that a mistake is committed by mistake. I supported the government once by killing my own people in a senseless war! I regretted it because the same government turned me into an outcast with poverty written all over my forehead.

AW: At least you are not as poor as you are making me to believe. You don't live in slums where the real poor people live.

KO: You have no right to say that my people live in slums! It is the people whom you serve that live in slums because, you see, their conscience is stained with the blood and sweat of the people. People who thrive on the blood of others are not fit to live in palaces!

AW: You talk as if I work as an errand boy! I am only doing my duty to my nation.

KO: Your duty, yes! But once you wear the garment of a thief, you become a thief; there's no honourable thief.

AW: Most times we teach others how to live when in fact we are the ones who need lessons on how to live.

KO: It is the corrupt government that you work for that needs lessons on how to lead ... how to govern!

AW: That is it! We condemn the devil every time and glorify the saints. We never pause to think that our judgment may be wrong because we never wait to hear the devil's own side of the story. Kenule, I do not want this interrogation session prolonged unnecessarily. You have taken too much levity already. The lives of two expatriates are in your hands, they must ...

KO: I don't know what you are talking about! And even if they are, the scale is not balanced. Just two lives, whereas they determine the course of our entire nation.

AW: But that should not make violence a means to route your grievances to ...

KO: What other ways do you proffer for people whose

voices cannot reach their leaders?

AW: Kenule, you need to be civil in your agitations!

KO: It is the government who must listen to the voice of the people!

AW: There are too many voices to listen to! The government cannot listen to every man on the streets. The transformation can only happen gradually.

KO: (*Mimicking.*) "The government cannot listen to every man on the street" ... I never said they should, but let them take a man from the streets and listen to his voice, see tears in his eyes and read frustration in his heart. That will be the resonance with which the suffering of our people can be measured.

AW: Kenule, for old times' sake, I implore you to tell me where you are keeping the two expatriates hostage. I promise you that I'll use my influence to get you amnesty from the government.

KO: I will not kowtow to your antics, and to that government to which you have pledged absolute loyalty.

AW: They are our government. We put them there with our votes. We must support them!

KO: (*Passionate.*) You are wrong. We do not put them there. The people we want never win, and if they do, they turn out to be people we don't want. Now, time and history have taught me that the first loyalty lies with my stomach and then my people. (*More* *passionately.*) A.S.P. Wariboko, have you forgotten? Has time erased the memories of the war from your head? The suffering? The hunger? The trauma of killing our own people? Do you remember the incident beside Orlu? I killed my own blood because of blind loyalty, despite his pleas; despite his cries. I thought I was doing the best thing for my country. (*Unconsciously play-acting the event.*) I remember vividly how it happened: "Hey you there, where do you think you're going?" The figure turned, and it was Ibeh, my mother's sister's son. I saw relief written all over his face when he recognized me: "Kenule, big boy soldier, so this is you?" He was coming to embrace me, but I stopped him with the barrel of my gun. "Why, Brother?" he asked. I told him there and then that we were no longer brothers. I warned him at the beginning of the crisis. I told him the national soldier held more hope than the sectional army. He refused to listen. He told me he could not leave his family, his tribe and expose all he had to danger. Then he joined the "rebel" soldiers. Yes, that was what we thought; everyone who was not with the national army was a "rebel". I could have allowed him to escape that day, but I was absolutely blinded with loyalty. My eyes were bloodshot. "Brother, you won't kill your kinsman because of a senseless war?" "Brother", "kinsman", "senseless"; those three words made me furious. I hit him with the butt of my gun. Then he sensed I was serious. He made a run for it. I put six shots through his back. I killed my blood, my own blood, because he was defending my people.

AW: No need for regrets now. Years have covered those scars and memories.

KO: No, Adolphus, that is where we go wrong! We need to atone. We need to seek forgiveness openly from God and man. Years after, that event still comes back to me; vivid. (*Weeps.*) Think of it. You shot a helpless man from the back. Six hot leads into the spine of a man who called you "brother".

AW: Yes, I recognize it's bad, but this is no moment for stirring emotions.

KO: There is no moment apportioned for truth. The truth must be said at all times.

AW: Yes, I know. War is sweet to only those who do not fight, but we have to forget about the memories of the war and face what we are here for.

KO: (*Smiles.*) Yes, I know why you wouldn't want to hear.

AW: Hear what? (*Brief silence, and then, moments of consternating recollection.*) No, no, don't talk about that …

KO: I don't blame you, Adolphus. I could have been part of it; I could have done it too … that frail girl … her breast defiantly upright — never been breached by the perilous hands of men. You took her to the bush, muffled her strength and forcefully took her. She couldn't resist because you had knocked her off. That devilish canal intrusion. You didn't even wait after the shame to see if she was alive.

AW: Our time is running out here!

KO: Adolphus, I am not blaming you for taking her. The senseless war provided an excuse for moral chaos. I could have followed you into the bush with her, but ... but I already killed a woman; my own mother. The peril of my birth was her unfortunate demise.

AW: I know so many bad things happened during the war. I have come to realize that war of any kind is dangerous to the existence of man. As our people would say, when the juju asks for blood sacrifice, you do not offer it palm oil.

KO: It is not only the war, Adolphus. Our inhumanity to one another. A government that is not sensitive to the suffering of its people.

AW: You always blame government, but do you know how much atrocity the common man himself commits every day?

KO: I know. You're right, friend. That is where our lessons will start from.

AW: So, why are you bothering the government every day when the people themselves are wicked to each other?

KO: You talk like this because you don't live where these people live. You don't till the land like they do. You don't wake early in the cold hazy morning to cast your net into the sea to find that all your fishes are dead. The dignity of these people is being crushed by people who have no stake in their lands.

AW: (*Sighs.*) Kenule, let us save that discussion for a friendly atmosphere. It is not within the ethical framework of my profession to leave gaps for digression. Their people are worried. The government is embarrassed. The national image is plunging. Where are you keeping them?

KO: I don't know anything about the kidnap.

A.W: (*Furiously jerking his collar.*) Of course, you do! If anything happens to them ... (*The two policemen rush in.*)

POLICEMEN: You called, Sir!

AW: Get out!

POLICEMEN: Yes, Sir! (*They leave.*)

AW: I wouldn't want you to take levity for granted.

KO: Yes, I know the line that cuts friendship from duty.

AW: Good.

KO: (*Patronizing him.*) For once you failed to bottle up your anger.

AW: It is not anger; it is part of my work, my duty.

KO: Yes, I remember. We learnt that in the army, too. To prey on innocent citizens in the line of our duties. Like the vultures, our friends during the war who were nourished daily from human corpses.

AW: Let us suspend the memories of war for now. Kenule, it is my duty to protect those expatriates you kidnapped and ...

KO: Save your government international embarrassment.

AW: Oh yes, you know.

KO: Tell me, what has the government done for you?

AW: What have you done for the country?

KO: This country doesn't belong to me. I used to think that the country belongs to all those who have made it their home; but no, it belongs only to a few. A registered few who have made it a hell for others. It is a place where our selfish leaders have destroyed all valuables of human construct.

AW: It still does not... (*Light goes off, leaving the stage in semi-darkness.*)

KO: (*Laughs.*) Yes, everything works here, but they never function.

AW: Even when there is light, the heart of the people thrives in darkness. It is not a problem for government alone, the people themselves must learn to love light, I mean in their hearts.

KO: Yes, in their hearts. (*Light comes on.*) That is if they still have hearts left.

AW: (*Glancing at his wristwatch.*) Kenule, you have thirty minutes to speak out before you are taken to the torture chamber.

KO: I have been tortured all my life. I find no fear in that threat.

AW: It is no threat! Kenule, right here, the friendship stops. When you are taken in there it becomes a different world entirely. I will not be there.

KO: (*Reflecting.*) The friendship? Oh yes, I remember. We used to be good friends during the war. Mutual. Do you still remember our secret deflections into the bush; communal fellowship with marijuana? The strands of our hairs erect, eyes bulged and reddened? And then, in those high moments, we would sing the anthem:

Nigeria we hail thee,
Our own dear native land;
Though tribe and tongue may differ,
In brotherhood we stand,
Nigerians all are proud to serve
Our sovereign Motherland.

Our flag shall be a symbol,
That truth and justice reign,
In peace or battle honour'd,
And this we count as gain,
To hand on to our children,
A banner without stain.

(ADOLPHUS *unconsciously joins him halfway through.*)

KO: And after the anthem, we would stand together side by side imitating the parade and the colour party, humming the song of the parade band and doing our mock march. (*They both go on a march. First marking time and then doing fast and slow time.* KENULE *disengages suddenly.)*

KO: Those were the periods of "friendship". It stopped after the war. Friendship stops when hearts no longer speak the same language.

AW: We are still friends, whichever way you see it. But, as I told you earlier, friendship and duty are clearly partitioned.

KO: Yes, I know.

AW: So, where are they?

KO: Who?

AW: The men!

KO: Which men?

AW: The expatriates!

KO: Which expatriates?

AW: The ones you kidnapped!

KO: Are you serious?

AW: I am dead serious, friend!

KO: You're funny!

AW: Well, we shall see!

KO: I did not kidnap those men!

AW: This is becoming interesting. I guess I may have to take you out without the hands of friendship. You are responsible for five violent protests and eight mischievous kidnappings in five years.

KO: Those demonstrations were never meant to be violent. They were staged to be peaceful, but hungry hoodlums took over. The hostage takings were meant to score particular points.

AW: What point could you have wanted to score without respect for the life and dignity of your fellow men ...?

KO: They are not my fellow men! They are foreigners. They plunder my people, destroy their environments and ...

AW: But violence and hostage-taking will not solve the problem!

KO: Yes, I know it will not, but I will not stand and watch the rape on my people! That was the only thing left that I could do for them. I once pointed the barrel of a gun at them. Bullets from my gun alone have felled hundreds of my own people. This is the only way to cover my shame, my betrayal.

AW: So, now you want to be a hero?

KO: No, I will never be. Not even an unsung hero. I am only paying the price of betrayal. I don't want to be a hero like the leaders you serve. Those who build monuments for themselves with the money meant for their people. They appear first as an inflated rubber ball; very taut. Then, a prick of needle on the ball and the gentle hissing deflation. Worn. They become worn heroes.

AW: We celebrate heroes from other parts of the world and leave ours unsung.

KO: Don't mistake giants for heroes. What you have

here are giants who throw you back to yesterday with unfulfilled promises.

AW: (*Reflecting.*) Yes, I remember that we talked so much about "heroes" and "giants" during the war.

KO: Yes "heroes" and "giants". And then I remember who used to be our hero.

AW: Our hero?

KO: Yes.

AW: (*Trying to remember.*) Our hero ...

KO: Che! You have forgotten? The man you admired so much. The one we spent our monies buying all the books about.

AW: Yes, Che.

KO: Che Guevara! The asthmatic Argentine doctor turned guerilla rebel. Remember him?

AW: Yes, "*Ernesto Guevara de la Serna*".

KO: The one we called "*Che, ve ve me bamunga bulanka*". The lion!

AW: Yes! "*Che, ve ve me bamunga bulanka*!" And that song by those Southern African singers we used to sing when we remember him.

KO: *Che Che Kule*!

AW: (*Excited.*) *Che Che Kule!*

KO: (*Sings.*) "*Che Che Kule*"
"*Che kofi sa*"

"Kofisa langa"
"Langa ti langa"
"Kumba le-le."

(ADOLPHUS *joins him, both doing some old-time war dances.*)

"Che Che Kule"
"Che kofisa"
"kofisa langa"
"Langa ti langa"
"Kumba le-le."

AW: (*Suddenly comes to himself.*) I hope we leave the trivial past behind and face ...

KO: You call the past "trivial?" That past is the reason you and I still grope in darkness. I do not mean for us to go back. All I say is that there are still unhealed wounds from that past. We must work to heal them.

AW: All your grievances may be just, but using a wrong to right a wrong is itself wrong. You may put them all on paper and forward them to the appropriate authorities.

KO: (*Smiles.*) My friend, the pen-man, he tried it. He put them all on papers. He appealed passionately for the rights of his people. What happened? He was hanged! It is a lie when you say that the pen is mightier than the sword!

AW: That was then. Things are changing now.

KO: "Things are changing now". But what about the memory of the past? Maybe tomorrow it will heal, but now ... for now! Adolphus, remember, our commanders during the war, with chests full of war ribbons ordering the shooting of innocent people, all because they dared to raise a shield to protect their own people. Those memories: haggard bundles of human flotsam. Shards of flesh and bones flying all about. Huts crammed with the skeletal form of dying children; children who would have grown to become leaders. Rotten milk from the breasts of decomposing women; women who would have become mothers of leaders ...

AW: Stop!

KO: (*Deranged.*) The acrid smell of chemical powder ... stench of human corpses, gory sights of dismembered men we used to know, unidentified mass of human tissues ...

AW: (*Completely bewildered.*) I say stop!

KO: (*Entranced.*) Festering sewers of iniquity ... smouldering pile of blackened rubble ... catalogues of disgusting debris ... only the vultures found their pots full of meats when they came home to roost.

AW: Are you done? Now, let me remind you that the day we made up our minds to become soldiers, that was the day death became inconsequential to us.

KO: That was the day we became blood-sucking hounds. Animals are better; they don't kill each other with impunity like we do. Even a butcher kills a goat because people eat its meat. Adolphus, we cannot continue with these anguish and destruction.

AW: Yes, I know.

KO: War never brings out the good in anybody. Only peace makes sense during war, nothing else ... You remember how fathers hoisted their son's biers on their shoulders? How gunshots tore apart the flabby breasts of old women ...?

AW: Oh, not again!

KO: The memory hurts.

AW: (*Changing the topic.*) Kenule Ododo, leader, Coastal Fighters Group, led five violent riots in ...

KO: You are giving me the name I don't bear.

AW: (*Looks at his watch.*) It is twenty minutes between you and the torture chamber.

KO: The torture chamber is designed for men.

AW: It is tactless, Kenule. After the torture, you'll still come to do what you should have done.

KO: There is nothing I will do that I have not done now.

AW: This act of terrorism will lead you nowhere.

KO: (*Defiantly.*) I am not a terrorist!

AW: Of course, you are!

KO: I am not!

AW: Shut up!

KO: (*Gapes.*) Oh ... Adolphus?

AW: I told you a line separates duty and friendship.

KO: Yes, I remember.

AW: Mr Kenule Ododo, where were you at 5:40 pm on Tuesday?

KO: The same place I was when I was arrested.

AW: Answer me straight!

KO: Our people say that it is what a man likes that kills him. I was at a beer joint in Burutu at that particular time.

AW: The expatriates were kidnapped at Forcados and every hint of suspicion points at you.

KO: (*Chuckles.*) Don't be confused, Adolphus. I couldn't be in Burutu and Forcados at the same time.

AW: It is possible, my friend. There is something we call "alibi". You make all necessary proofs to be in a place, yet perpetrating a crime somewhere else.

KO: Then the proper name for it should be magic; black power.

AW: It is no joking matter, Kenule, your time is slipping out of my hands. The international community is watching. The stability of our democracy is under threat.

KO: Our democracy has never been stable: It is the scrotum of a madman. It swings restlessly.

AW: Look, remember we fought that war so that we can have a united nation.

KO: The reason for the war was lost before it began.

We shouldn't have fought that war. We shouldn't have raised arms against each other. Now we are more disunited as a nation. Our leaders are bosses. But as you know, a good leader ought to lead from behind, letting the weak and the feeble also have their say.

AW: At about 9.30 pm you left the drinking joint …

KO: So you have found out?

AW: Where did you go to?

KO: You ought to know.

AW: (*Firmly.*) Where did you go to!

KO: I said you ought …

AW: (*Slaps him.*) Answer me!

KO: (*Holding his ears.*) I have known you for thirty years, and you raised your hands against me.

AW: (*Not flattered.*) I asked; where did you go when you left the drinking joint!

KO: (*Shaken.*) To my house.

AW: Liar! You left for somewhere else, not your house!

KO: Yes, I went for a meeting with my group.

AW: Where?

KO: We are under oath not to disclose our point of meetings.

AW: I guessed as much. So when did you come back?

KO: From where?

AW: When did you return from your meeting to your house!

KO: Sometime early in the morning.

AW: After you had properly secured your hostages?

KO: I was no party to that hostage-taking.

AW: Maybe you're not, but it's your group who is keeping them hostage.

KO: I am the leader of the group; I dictate all our modes of action.

AW: (*Sarcastic.*) You "dictate" all your modes of action, and then you turn around and start shouting democracy.

KO: My people do not complain.

AW: They don't need to! What I mean is that you don't live what you fight for. It is ironic how much we blame our leaders for every ill in the nation but we perpetrate more of those ills among ourselves.

KO: I can see that they are really paying you well for image laundering.

AW: Now back to business. You were not there at the point of kidnapping according to you, but I can say that you "dictated" the instruction.

KO: I do not know anything about what you are saying.

AW: On the other hand, it is very possible that you never "dictated" the instruction to your people, but acting on impulse and loyalty to you, they carried out the kidnapping.

KO: My group will take no such action without my knowledge.

AW: Kenule, you had better open up to me. I am your friend.

KO: (*Musingly.*) Yes, friend ... you are my friend.

AW: And your brother as well.

KO: Yes, "brother". That same word. That word we use so often but never know its meaning.

AW: We will always be brothers, Kenule. Remember those days at primary school. Our forays to the river bank of Nun. You and I, and Bina — God bless his memory. Those old times that we shared have put us under one spell of brotherhood.

KO: Then duty came and the cord of brotherhood snapped.

AW: Remember that we both agreed to join the national army as brothers.

KO: We were young then. We thought we were doing the right thing. We thought killing our own brothers was the same thing as keeping the country together.

AW: That was our yesterday. We don't need to regret it now.

KO: It was indeed yesterday; the yesterday that was so full of unfulfilled promises.

AW: Kenule Ododo, in the name of the law, where are

you keeping them?

KO: You asked earlier in the name of "brotherhood", I told you I knew nothing about it. You don't expect me to say otherwise now that you asked in the name of the law; your law, which I hold in disregard.

AW: You and your group once kidnapped five expatriates, and you denied it.

KO: There was no sense in that denial, that was why we released them without hassles. We vowed thenceforth to take responsibility for our actions.

AW: You don't expect me to fall for that?

KO: Of course I don't. It is part of your duty not to trust a word from the mouth of a suspect — even if he is a friend and a brother.

AW: You keep mixing duty and friendship.

KO: No, I stopped when that slap landed on my face.

AW: I am quite sorry about that ...

KO: You don't need to! I would have done the same thing if the situation were the other way round. It was the same reason I killed my own blood in a senseless war. We called ourselves patriots then, taking delight in seeing the mangled flesh of human corpses.

AW: You're traumatized, Brother.

KO: I am not. I just look back in anger at those senseless moments. I imagine the endless impossibility of wars all the world round. Today, brothers are taking arms against brothers. Nations are rising against one another. The strength of big nations is measured by how many destructive weapons there are in their arsenals. They suffocate the future before it comes. Yet, smaller nations are being harassed when they follow their footsteps. Some human animals profit from these endless massacres, genocides and bloody vendettas, while the weak count their sorrows. And then, tomorrow, we all sit at a table and call one another "brother".

AW: Sometimes, war is a matter of necessity.

KO: No war is necessary, Friend! Every war fought, every weapon of death that we point at each other is an abuse of humanity! It was an eternal regret when I came to terms with the truth that my gun sent my fellow men to their early graves. That is the reason my group remains the only non-violent group in the coast.

AW: Except when the group decides to riot?

KO: They were hoodlums that took over and hijacked our cause.

AW: That may have been the case for now: a planned hostage-taking hijacked by ... by a disgruntled portion of your group.

KO: I know nothing about what you are saying.

AW: It is possible we are saying the same thing. Without your knowledge, some members of your group decided to ...

KO: My group is not responsible for the kidnapping!

AW: Let us do it this way; what were the issues discussed at the meeting that night?

KO: I can't remember now.

AW: What if you try, even if it's a little detail?

KO: I cannot remember. They were all written down in the minutes.

AW: Can I get a look at the minutes?

KO: It is not with me.

AW: I know. I mean can you help me get it?

KO: It is not in my custody.

AW: Who is having it?

KO: My personal secretary. And don't bother yourself asking who he is, or looking for him. He is faceless. You will never know him.

AW: (*Sighs.*) I guess so. Kenule, I believe so much that you'll be willing to sacrifice some information for your freedom. You should be at home with your children.

KO: Home? Stop kidding, Adolphus. We have no homes, you and I. Have you forgotten? (*Soberly.*) Remember! Remember our anxiety when we learnt that the war would soon be over. Our plans. Our vision. Then the announcement came: "The war is ended!" It was time for reconciliation, reconstruction and rehabilitation. We jubilated and sang! (*Sings.*):

Oh my home
Oh my home
When shall I see my home?
When shall I see my native land?
I will never forget my home.

But we were wrong! We found out days after the war that there was really nowhere to go. We had destroyed our homes with shellings. Some of us were no longer the same men who left their homes years back for the war. We have lost it, Adolphus. Those homes can no longer shelter us.

AW: That is one problem with you; empty ideologies. You're a failed activist, Kenule. Don't you understand that?

KO: It is you who don't understand! It is you who need to know that killing one another and calling it "duty" or "patriotism" is wrong!

AW: That was in the war. Now, I am a policeman and my duty is to protect human lives, not to take them!

KO: Yes, but how many of your people really do that? You kill innocent people with customized impunity, brandishing flowery languages to the world. You justify wrong actions by modifying language: "in the line of duty", "accidental discharge", "stray bullets", "suspects" and so on and so forth.

AW: It is unreasonable to condemn what you don't understand.

KO: What about the harassment of innocent citizens on the streets? What about the various clamping into detentions without trial? The puppet tools you play in the hands of our desperate leaders? And when you are sated, we all sit together over bottles of beer and call one another "brothers". This is not the country we both dreamt of. This is not why we went to war. This is not why we both conspired and killed that white man, Major Robertson — the British mercenary. Remember him? We killed him at Ogoja for spitting on our people and our nation. He called us "idiots" and "natives", we swallowed that. Then he called our country "dark" and "crude". That lump was too much to swallow. We shot him at the back inside the bush at Ogoja. He was supposed to be our battalion commander, but we killed him. And then Corporal Sylvanus began to suspect. He asked why enemy bullets would pass our backs without hitting us before coming to Major Robertson. He asked why the bullets would hit him at the back when he was facing us and the bullets were coming from the west. We knew we had not covered our ground very well. The only choice was to kill Sylvanus, too. You pumped those bullets into his skull. I still see the way his brain scattered into the air.

AW: (*Sore.*) Don't invoke ugly memories here!

KO: That is what I am saying, Adolphus. We need to atone for that past and work for a good future. That cannot be done when the same people march boldly to our land to tap our oil, killing all our fishes and leaving us with nothing but crumbs.

AW: Yes I know, but ...

KO: There is no "but" in the matter, my friend. Imagine you are a woman and a stranger walks boldly to your house and takes you forcefully, and then takes away the wrapper that shelters you from cold. It is wrong!

AW: Yes.

KO: They take our oil and leave all our farms ruined. They leave all our fishes dead. The air we breathe gets corrupt and they take our people for cheap labour. They take away everything that puts food on the table of my people.

AW: This thing belongs to everybody; it is a common wealth.

KO: I am not saying it isn't, all I fight for is that these people deserve to live like human beings. A little more to better their lives will not cause a quarrel.

AW: You make me laugh. Do you know how much is remitted to your leaders every month to develop your land? It is them you should ask where all the monies go to.

KO: We are compiling a list of their names. When we finish, we shall go for them one by one.

AW: (*Brief silence.*) Now to business. Tell me, how much is your ransom?

KO: I don't understand what you mean.

AW: How much are you demanding to release your hostages!

KO: There are no hostages on my hands.

AW: I suppose you will not yield easily.

KO: I tell you, I know nothing about any hostages.

AW: (*Glances at his wristwatch.*) Each second ticks you to the torture room.

KO: (*Smiles.*) I told you earlier, there is no greater torture than living a life of want, a life of quest. That room you threaten me with was designed for men.

AW: I mean, there is no need … it is useless waiting to be tortured before saying the truth.

KO: Stop threatening me!

AW: I am not threatening you!

KO: You are!

AW: I am only telling you what you'll face!

KO: Let me face it!

AW: Stop shouting!

KO: I am not shouting!

AW: You are!

KO: I am not …!

AW: Shut up! (*Brief silence.*) I may not need to apologize for doing my duty.

KO: I understand.

AW: I guess you will. I told you earlier …

KO: A line separates friendship and duty.

AW: Yes, now you know.

KO: And patriotism severs the cord of brotherhood.

AW: In your opinion.

KO: And now the torture chamber.

AW: No, not now. You still have some few minutes. You might be able to help yourself and me by answering some few questions.

KO: I thought I have answered all your questions?

AW: No, you have avoided every one of them. You don't understand how much I am trying to help you as a friend. I am ...

KO: Don't cross your boundary, Adolphus. Forget friendship for now and face your duty.

AW: You need to forget that we share different opinions.

KO: Don't be a hypocrite, Brother. We have always shared the same opinion and ideology during the war and after. Tell me you don't want a country where everyone has food on their tables, good clothes to wear and decent shelter over their heads? Adolphus, tell me you don't want a peaceful country with the basic amenities of life, where one and each could develop their lives and contribute to the future of their children? That is the opinion we both shared, but now ... I don't blame you; sometimes we have to stop being ourselves to put food in our stomachs. You have covered those ideas with those of your reckless leaders whose orders you cannot refuse.

AW: You were in the force, mind you, no one refuses an order from a superior officer.

KO: I know. That is why I don't blame you. Left alone, with food on your table, you will choose a nobler way to serve the nation.

AW: I would still have chosen the police; there is no nobler way than this to serve the nation.

KO: You get me wrong there. I am talking about the system, not the profession. Remember the army had appealed to us as a noble profession even before the war. It was a place of hope and opportunity then for us to contribute to the development of our nation, but ...

AW: The various intrigues among the rank and file.

KO: It was terrible! It destroyed the fabric of unity among the soldiers and led to that senseless war. The same thing is with the police. Our people now spite them. They will rather run to embrace a leper than shake a man in police uniform.

AW: It is not that bad.

KO: You think it isn't?

AW: It can never be that bad.

KO: I see ... (*Smirks.*) I hope so.

AW: We should not always hammer on our bad sides, this country still nurtures some hope.

KO: With changes, with new crops of ideal leaders.

AW: You have lost faith completely in our present leaders. You don't see anything good about them.

KO: All my life I had had faith in them. With each appearance, they smashed that faith. I killed my brother because of the faith I had in them. I realized after the war that I was not only wrong, I was stupidly insane. Those leaders I had faith in turned me into an outcast. They made yesterday claim my past, they made history condemn my future.

AW: You are still vindictive about that war. That war was fought several years ago.

KO: My grievance is not only for the war, it is also for the present. Even those soldiers who did not die during the war have died every day after; slow deaths, from hunger and want. Our men who lost their lives during the war ... remember Captain Shehu Dan-Daura, that elegant soldier, knocked out at Uli. What did they do for him? In the bush they arranged a rapid funeral programme; brisk walking soldier undertakers, body rolled into a rough four feet hole, and the soldier reverend: "May the peace of the Lord be with you till we meet again. A gallant soldier who served his country with utmost loyalty. A patriot. May your gentle soul rest in perfect peace, amen". And then the song:

Sleep on beloved
Sleep and take thy rest
Lay down thy head
Upon the saviour's breast

We love thee well
But Jesus loves thee best
Goodnight! Goodnight! Goodnight!

And that was all, committed to eternal forgetfulness. His family is still languishing in want. There are still many disabled war veterans at the rehabilitation centre at Oji River; one zinc shanty encampment housing people that should be treated as heroes.

AW: We are victims, too.

KO: That's what I am telling you.

AW: But that's past, the government cannot do anything about that.

KO: They may not do anything about the past, but they can make life suitable for living now. You don't understand. That is the only way to forget the past.

AW: And ...

KO: That is what I am fighting for. Not for myself, but for the generation coming. That is the only contribution I can make to their future.

AW: Yes, but it takes time. The fabric holding us together is torn. We need patience to mend it. You were right when you talked about my ideas for our country. I have come to discover a secret; we cannot stop them at a go. The process will have to be gradual.

KO: The common man has exercised too much patience. They have clipped our mouths for long by pointing guns at us. It is difficult to keep your dignity in poverty. Now, it is time to trade our lives for freedom.

AW: Fire for fire will leave everybody burnt. All that will be left is ashes.

KO: Yes … and from the ashes our country can spring up a new life. (*Demonstrating.*) Like the phoenix which rose from the rubble, it will rise to shake off the ashes and start a new life, stronger, bigger and tougher. It is now ready to fight off all its oppressors in its renewed vitality.

AW: You're contradicting yourself; you told me some minutes back that you are an apostle of non-violence.

KO: You are the one who contradicts the meaning. Non-violence does not mean stupid passivity when you're oppressed. It means taking your time to attack the agents of oppression.

AW: Kenule, it is minutes between you and the …

KO: The torture chamber.

AW: It is no threat, my brother.

KO: It is duty.

AW: Those expatriates have committed no crime.

KO: It is a crime when you plunder people's wealth and leave their land depleted.

AW: But they were licensed to do that!

KO: Licensed to plunder?

AW: No, I mean licensed to tap the oil.

KO: Licensed by whom?

AW: Licensed by whom?

KO: Yes, licensed by whom?

AW: Licensed by ... look, friend, we don't have the license to discuss that here!

KO: We can't afford not to discuss it because, you see, my people keep asking why they should be set back by the wealth they produce. They have the license to ask questions!

AW: But there is a formula...

KO: "Formulas", "measures", "reforms", "palliatives", "vision", "transformation", those are the things we hear every time, but the common man still goes hungry.

AW: We need a bit of patience to grow.

KO: Patience is all we shout to the common man. Those who are supposed to be our leaders continue to steal and steal! And to us, they shout patience. "The dividends of democracy can only be garnered if we exercise patience". Patience my foot!

AW: If every other man on the street sounds the way you sound, we may be going back to another war.

KO: If there will be another war, it will be between the common man and those who have drawn the hands of our clock back; between the common man and the robbers we call leaders. We shall not go back to those senseless killings to leave our children in ...

AW: Yes, the children!

KO: The children will be ...

AW: No, I'm not talking about war. I mean ... you may have a different case to answer from this. Your group has a ridiculous number of the under-aged as militias. The whole world frowns at such abuse of children.

KO: Don't judge my group with the world's reaction! I am Kenule Ododo — the leader of Coastal Fighters Group! I fight for the people of the coast alone, not the world!

AW: You are raising your voice!

KO: I fight for the right of my people!

AW: (*Shouting him down.*) I said you are raising your voice! (*The two policemen rush in.*)

POLICEMEN: You called, Sir?

AW: Get out!

POLICEMEN: Yes, Sir!

AW: Come back! Don't you step your bloody feet in here until you are called!

POLICEMEN: Yes, Sir! (*They leave.*)

AW: Yes, back to the point I was making. Your group is notorious for arming children for hostilities.

KO: It is their wish.

AW: No! It cannot be their wish. You took them from their mothers.

KO: Those children walked into the group with their legs. Nobody forced them to join.

AW: We are still saying the same thing. Mere admittance into your fold is a serious crime against humanity.

KO: I can't stop them if they desire to defend their motherland.

AW: Of course, you can stop them! Young children of fourteen and fifteen years; imagine if they were your children? You teach them to use dangerous weapons thereby turning them into terrorists.

KO: They believe in the spirit of the struggle. These children will take over when we are gone.

AW: You are holding tight to your opinion as if it's right. This exploitation of children in armed hostilities does irrevocable harm to them and it destroys the future for all. It is robbing our people of the future leaders they will need to advance our society.

KO: They have chosen the path ...

AW: You're wrong, don't you understand? What you're doing is a crime against man and God! You place carbines in their hands instead of pens. You make them spread death even when they are yet to understand the meaning of life!

KO: So, I turn them away when they come to enlist?

AW: You turn them away! In fact there should be rigid provisions which must spell out age limits. These children are being deprived of the opportunity to live a normal life.

KO: (*Silence.*) Maybe you're right. I shall begin to work on it when I leave here.

AW: You may not leave here as easily as you dreamed.

KO: Oh yes, I was forgetting the torture chamber.

AW: We may not need to go that far. This thing is simple: just a little information on the kidnapping.

KO: I don't know a thing about the kidnapping.

AW: You're getting on my nerves, Kenule.

KO: I should tell you that, Adolphus. I have been here for three days, and it's the same question all through.

AW: You have kept yourself here for three days! We could have been through with this a long time.

KO: Yes, we could have been through with it before Christ; through with it, and after, you'll walk back to your table, and I to jail.

AW: I told you it would be easier than you imagined. I shall use my influence to make things easy for you.

KO: Like?

AW: Amnesty, state pardon …

KO: (*Chuckles.*) So, so funny.

AW: What is funny?

KO: When you talk about using your influence for me, I was thinking if I admitted that I was responsible for the kidnapping, you'll organize a cocktail party for me at a five-star hotel.

AW: Don't be ridiculous, Kenule, I mean …

KO: Arrest, detention, harassment …

AW: It may not be the way you think.

KO: How do you mean? Your government doesn't go about shaking hands with terrorists and inviting them for dinner?

AW: It may not be that way either.

KO: Then tell me what way it is.

AW: You will have to tell me where you've kept them before we talk about that.

KO: Kept who?

AW: The men.

KO: Which men?

AW: Come on, Ken, we don't want to go over all that again.

KO: I don't understand what you're talking about.

AW: Kenule, time! Time is not on our side!

KO: "Time is not on our side". You fear to see a friend being led into the torture chamber?

AW: That place is horrible!

KO: I was in the army, remember. I was shot and kidnapped by enemy soldiers. Torture has been my companion since the day my mother bore me.

AW: Don't talk like that.

KO: Let me talk like this, Adolphus. I have been tortured all my life. I have known hunger and want all my life. I remember those fishes we trapped at the bank of River Nun to rekindle life. The luggage we both used to carry at the port in Forcados to earn a few coins for our upkeep. We even tried to send ourselves to school. Remember? Kenule and Adolphus, raft boys at Burutu: "Hey, sail the raft here and load these goods on the raft and have these coins for your effort." Those were days of torture. While our brothers were learning in school, we were learning to become men outside. We became men before our time, but we lost the privilege to grow.

AW: (*Irritated.*) Memories! Memories! All you can do is to excite memories...!

KO: And the church lent its own tortures, too, its own deceit. We would pray to Saint Peter, Saint Joseph and Virgin Mary and sing "Ave Maria". The white Reverend with his continuous refrain, "Never judge a man by his colour". We would look round. There was only one white face among the congregation aside the reverend father himself — his wife! The other whites in the district had no time for church. They had only three obsessions: booze, fish and women.

AW: Those memories ...

KO: The church took away our pastimes, our adventures at the back of the Niger: looking at the seaweeds, hearing the gentle laps of water against the rocks, catching those crabs stunned by the surf and collecting the conch shells which the waves brought in from far away. You remember that day when we had our first voyage on the river inside the canoe with an outboard engine? That had been our dream for years. We were so happy! We never knew that happiness and sorrow are like changing seasons; they are never permanent. Then the war came, and we joined the army to escape the torture. That was our greatest mistake. The war battered us and turned out to be the worst torture a man could encounter. Those guns we held gave us power. But it was the power that kept our people in bondage.

AW: That doesn't count any longer.

KO: It doesn't but the never-ending struggle with oneself, with the past, with the present, with the leaders, in fact with everything!

AW: Don't get vindictive over everything. You might lose your mind.

KO: I am still searching for my mind. I lost it several years back.

AW: (*Suddenly adopting a formal stance.*) Mr Kenule Ododo, Leader, Coastal Fighters Group, where have you kept them?

KO: I guess I have little time before the torture chamber.

AW: Where have you kept them?

KO: Kept who?

AW: (*Jerks him up.*) Answer me! Where have you kept them?

KO: When I look into those eyes, I find it difficult to imagine they belong to a man who once called me brother.

AW: I will not be taken in by that flimsy patronage!

KO: I am not patronizing you.

AW: Where have you kept them?

KO: I don't know about them.

AW: You do, man, you do!

KO: Don't get worked up.

AW: I'm not worked up!

KO: You are.

AW: I am not, friend!

KO: I can see it.

AW: It's my duty I'm doing!

KO: Patriot.

AW: Don't joke with me!

KO: I am not.

AW: So tell me what I want to know!

KO: You're wasting your time.

AW: (*Quietly, menacingly.*) You're headstrong. After the torture, you might be walking straight into jail.

KO: I know.

AW: So, why are you doing this to yourself?

KO: Doing what?

AW: Come on, where is your brain, Man?

KO: (*Points to his head.*) Inside this skull.

AW: It's not there! It's not there, Man! If it's there you'll do the right thing.

KO: Like?

AW: Like confiding in me, telling me all there is so that I can help.

KO: Do you think I trust you?

AW: You have to, so that I can help you.

KO: Stop kidding, Friend. I don't trust you.

AW: We're friends, and brothers. If you don't trust me, who else is there to trust?

KO: (*Smiles.*) I stopped trusting you during the war. You remember the horrible incident at Ore?

AW: (*Visibly shaken.*) Don't start!

KO: That is why I will never trust you, my brother. You think I have forgotten? No. That incident comes back to me every day. I begged you not to … there was already a ceasefire. We had routed the village into surrendering, but you went ahead …

AW: I say don't!

KO: You killed him, Adolphus, despite my pleas. You killed him because of the money.

AW: The money was discovered and later seized from me.

KO: It doesn't matter. That incident left me with a lesson: never trust your friend or brother absolutely.

AW: It has nothing to do with you, Kenule.

KO: You could kill me because of money, too.

AW: Don't say that. You're my friend and ...

KO: Whatever you do to others, you can do to your friend, and brother.

AW: And to think of it, there was war during that period.

KO: Yes. But we use wars as excuse to remit the crimes in our heart.

AW: That incident was my worst nightmare.

KO: (*Reflecting.*) That young man. Probably all the rewards of his hard work. He was happy he survived the war. Then he looked back and got strangled.

AW: Please don't remind me anymore!

KO: Friend, you see why we need to go back? Why we need to look into the past, into those mistakes and atone for them?

AW: I sought forgiveness in a church years after.

KO: It is not enough, Brother. Have you ever thought of going back to that house where you killed him, to know if any compensation could be given, to know if he had any family?

AW: Hum … I …

KO: I went to Ibeh's grave. I knelt and sought his forgiveness. I cleansed myself of his blood. When we wrong each other, it shouldn't be difficult for us to say sorry.

AW: You're right. It shouldn't be hard for us to say we're sorry. But more importantly, the past shouldn't be a reason to distrust your brother.

KO: Trust is a fragile cord. Once it breaks, it breaks. If you try to mend it, the scar leaves a horrible picture.

AW: Yes, Kenule, and we're all victims.

KO: And that is why we need to correct those ugly mistakes of the past so that we can tender a good future before our children.

AW: And that was why I eventually joined the police.

KO: The same reason why I founded my group.

AW: (*Overreacts.*) The group was responsible for five violent riots under five years!

KO: I told you those demonstrations started peacefully!

AW: And?

KO: They were hijacked by hungry hoodlums, miscreants, urchins!

AW: So you could not control the monster you created?

KO: We tried to avoid violent clashes in town. Those hoodlums ...

AW: To avoid confrontations with the hoodlums, you allowed the houses of innocent citizens to be burnt, their shops broken into and goods looted.

KO: There was no reason for violent clashes which could claim lives.

AW: Well, that is no point to discuss now. Let us come back to the present.

KO: Yes, the present; only that the ugliness of the past will not give way.

AW: You keep talking about the past, don't you think about the future? Talk about tomorrow?

KO: Tomorrow?

AW: Yes, let's talk about tomorrow. We shouldn't allow the ugly past to deter the future.

KO: You're right. In the same way we shouldn't allow the future to be blurred by the mistakes of the past.

AW: We need to look up, look into the rising sun and work together for a better nation.

KO: And again be turned out in the end like outcasts?

AW: Nobody turned you out, Kenule!

KO: The nation turned me out! Her leaders turned me out in shame. After the war, I had no shoes, I had no shelter, no clothes and I could barely feed myself!

We fought that war to have a better country, but it was worse after the war. You could see wealth around you, but they were not meant for you, no matter how hard you worked. It was those who found themselves in the position of leadership that owned the wealth.

AW: Those were days gone by, the new government will ...

KO: There is nothing new about the government! You only watch but you don't see! Can't you see it's still the old government in disguise? Can't you see!

AW: Whatever government they are, we can't keep complaining. We need to contribute our own to lift the nation up.

KO: I will lift my people up first.

AW: That is too bad. This nation belongs to all of us.

KO: I felled my people once with my gun because I wanted to lift my nation up. Today, my voice cannot reach the ears of those I fought for. And you want me to turn around and make the same mistake?

AW: It is never a mistake to serve your country!

KO: And it is never a mistake for my country not to care for me! It is never a mistake for my country not to provide job and welfare system for me? No power, no job, no food! There is not even sense again for the common man! Have you been to Kasto lately? The running stream that cuts the town into two is still what people drink!

AW: I learnt government awarded a contract for a dam?

KO: They did, but you know better the government you serve. The award was only on paper; never meant to be executed. The money allocated for it must be resting in some personal accounts.

AW: We are in a terrible situation. This is one reason why you and I must lend our hands, sound our voices, so that we don't go back to the past.

KO: I don't trust the government.

AW: Even now?

KO: Yes.

AW: So whom do you want to trust? You don't trust your friend, your brother, government and …

KO: Myself.

AW: I was going to say that.

KO: I don't trust myself. When you look around and find there is nobody to trust, you get confused and begin to doubt even yourself.

AW: You confuse me.

KO: Oh! You doubt yourself too?

AW: No, not that, but I am thinking … I am thinking how many of us call others "thieves" when we ourselves are thieves.

KO: That is why I doubt myself.

AW: Most of us abuse government and call it names of all kinds, but if we occupy those seats, we will be worse.

KO: That's right. But government shouldn't wait until people complain and call it names before it ventures to improve their living standard.

AW: (*Glances at his wristwatch.*) I think ...

KO: My time is up?

AW: Pardon?

KO: Lead me to the torture chamber.

AW: You're not to give us instruction here on how to operate!

KO: I am sorry.

AW: Now, Kenule, what is the strength of your group?

KO: Strength?

AW: I mean how many are you?

KO: Our number shouldn't be a source of worry. We are not preparing to wage a war.

AW: This is an interrogation session, and I will want you to take it as such; no question is irrelevant.

KO: Alright, go on.

AW: How many are you in your group?

KO: People keep joining every day.

AW: What is the exact number?

KO: One thousand, six hundred.

AW: One thousand, six hundred! That is quite a number.

KO: That was when I left three days ago.

AW: So, some new members would have joined?

KO: I expect so.

AW: Do you expect to have disgruntled elements or rebels among you?

KO: No.

AW: And you're sure?

KO: I am sure.

AW: I hope you stop contradicting yourself. The other time you told me you trust nobody, now you're sure your group has no rebels.

KO: Rebellion has nothing to do with trust.

AW: So you trust them, then.

KO: I told you I have no friendship with trust.

AW: Good. Now, as a matter of assumption, a fraction of your group colludes and eventually kidnaps these expatriates without your knowledge. When the news gets to you, how will you feel?

KO: I would feel like I am feeling now.

AW: How?

KO: Normal.

AW: (*Sighs.*) Now let me assume you have knowledge of the kidnapping.

KO: Which I don't have.

AW: Assumption! I am assuming!

KO: I forgot.

AW: Yes, so after the kidnapping, how would you treat them?

KO: Treat who?

AW: The victims!

KO: Normal.

AW: Normal, like how?

KO: Like friends.

AW: Suppose any harm comes to them?

KO: I would not allow that.

AW: Now imagine one of them tries to escape. Will you shoot him?

KO: No.

AW: Why?

KO: Because he can't escape.

AW: How do you mean?

KO: When you take hostages, you take them to destination "zero", where they can neither help themselves nor get help.

AW: That is interesting. So I am to assume by your logic that the people being held hostage are presently helpless.

KO: You're right, but not by my logic. It is the logic of all those who take part in skilful kidnappings.

AW: Good. Now to assume you want to negotiate the release of people held captives by hostages, how would you go about it?

KO: I have never found myself on that side. When I do, my gumption will bail me out.

AW: Nice thought. But come to think of it, those people being held captives, most of them are here on genuine business.

KO: Genuine business?

AW: Yes! Most of them only turned out to be what they are because your people prompted and encouraged them.

KO: You don't want to take it that these people are plunderers?

AW: They are plunderers because your people plundered with them! Imagine this. Do you think they have the guts to do what they are doing if some of your people don't profit from their gains?

KO: Maybe you're right.

AW: It is not maybe. I am definitely right. Then the people who wanted to be part of them but had no opportunity turn themselves into their enemies, terrorizing them in the course of their business ...

KO: I believe that allusion was not meant for my group.

AW: It is meant for any group who takes law into its hands and boycotts the legitimate course of routing grievances.

KO: Adolphus, you don't know these people! They don't understand the language of dialogue. They have so much protection and power that the only means to get their attention is to seize their attention.

AW: But then violence...

KO: Stop calling these actions violence! Do you know how much violence these people commit against my people? Do you know how much of their land and fishes are destroyed every day?

AW: The mirror tells you the truth about yourself. These people you fight for are lazy! Because their land breeds oil, they take it as a means to be idle, not to develop other areas of their God-given potentials. I tell you, if you drive everybody away from those lands, and leave the people to their lands, they will do greater harm to one another.

KO: Is that the reason for their maltreatment?

AW: Nobody is maltreating your people.

KO: Our people! They are your people, too!

AW: (*Reluctantly.*) Our people. But the fact still remains that we cannot bury the truth because they are my people.

KO: There is no truth in what you are saying.

AW: Maybe if you have a little patience, and listen, you'll realize that we are both speaking the same thing, the same language, only at different levels of temperament.

KO: So you think we will ever speak the same language again?

AW: Kenule, our duties aside, the vision we have for our country must not die. That is the language we have always spoken together.

KO: *(Irate.)* Our country! You keep saying "our country". I tell you that this country is not for me!

AW: This country is for all of us.

KO: It is not for me! It is for those who sit there! It is for those who call themselves humans and turn us into slaves! It is for those who have food to eat and waste, not minding that some of us eat from the dustbin! It is for those who come to us on their knees proclaiming to have no shoes only to get to the position of leadership and become robbers!

AW: But that is no reason to say that you don't belong to this country. Every other nation in the world that we look up to had gone through such stages. For instance, America and ...

KO: Don't preach history to me! It does happen in the phase of development of most nations, I know, but that of my own country is too much, too long and too pathetic!

AW: That is why we all need to join hands and stop it!

KO: Join hands with who?

AW: Join hands with one another and the government, so that we can move the country forward.

KO: Stop dreaming. This government doesn't need your hand. Like your voice, it is too frail to make any impact. I told you earlier, this is no new government. It is still the same government that thrives on the sweat of its people.

AW: If I pretend to buy your argument — I mean assume that it's true, do we look on and not take up action?

KO: I have taken up the action I deem fit.

AW: Such action will only impede our ideas, destroy that future that we have both shared.

KO: We shared those ideas then. Now we no longer speak the same language. That is what you should get straight!

AW: Even if we do not speak the same language, we are held under the spell of oneness.

KO: You seem to have forgotten all the pains of the war, all the trauma, and the eventual betrayal by those we called leaders.

AW: I understand, but we have to move forward. It is easier to fall when you keep looking back. That past was a phase. We were all victims, but the promise of a better future washes away the pains of the past.

KO: Are you sure we can wash away the pains of that past?

AW: That past is a mere memory.

KO: It is not mere memory! The same people keep coming and coming to destroy our lives, and they call themselves our leaders.

AW: We shall overcome them. It's just that we need to take some time to study the situation, and then ...

KO: Strike!

AW: Just like Ehud ... in the Bible, the book of Judges: (*Acting out the situation.*) "And Ehud came unto him; and he was sitting in a parlour, which he had for himself alone. And Ehud said, "I have a message from God unto thee". And he arose out of his seat. And Ehud put forth his left hand, and took the dagger from his right thigh, and thrust it into his belly: And the handle also went in after the blade; and the fat closed upon the flesh, so that he could not draw the dagger out of his belly; and the dirt came out."

KO: The dirt of corruption, injustice and tyranny. What a beautiful escapade! The only problem is my preference for David; he did not hide under the cloak of a false messenger of God. He confronted Goliath face-to-face.

AW: Goliath underestimated David. That was why David got him. Nowadays, every Goliath has learnt his lessons; David may not be that lucky again.

KO: Now it is you who is being prophetic.

AW: It is the truth. We don't need a prophet to see it.

KO: So we strike?

AW: No, we're not striking yet, we need to come together and build the nation. Then we'll flush out the oppressors.

KO: Time! That will take a lot of time!

AW: Not too long. You just have patience. Remember, today is the tomorrow we talked about yesterday.

KO: But these people will continue to ...

AW: You must have faith that after darkness light will come. After rain comes sunshine. It doesn't take long for a flowing stream to break its barrier.

KO: To have something to eat, something to put on our bodies and a place to sleep at night should not be an issue we should always fight about, they are things that should never provoke controversy.

AW: Don't worry, Brother, we are a stone's-throw to freedom.

KO: *(Cogitates.)* Stone's-throw to freedom?

AW: Yes, freedom, for you and me. For all the ordinary men that walk in the streets.

KO: Yes, freedom!

AW: Freedom in its true sense!

KO: (*Excitedly.*) Yes, freedom!

AW: Freedom for all!

KO: For all of us!

AW: Now, Kenule, can we talk about the men you have...you are keeping?

KO: (*Slumps into the chair.*) My God! I thought we had finished with that?

AW: That's why we're both here, we need to talk about it and come to an agreement.

KO: What kind of agreement?

AW: Something that will benefit you and I. Look, we have already spent much time here, we need ...

KO: Adolphus?

AW: Yes.

KO: Will you trust me?

AW: Yes.

KO: As a brother and friend?

AW: Yes.

KO: I know nothing about the men who were kidnapped.

AW: Do you think I believe that?

KO: You said you will trust me.

AW: You warned me that trust is a fragile cord.

KO: Yes, but it only becomes a fragile cord after a betrayal.

AW: Very well. Can we talk about those men?

KO: I am listening.

AW: Where have you kept them?

KO: That is a bad start.

AW: Alright, alright ... what is the information you can give to me about them?

KO: Nothing.

AW: This is not fair. Ken, you are making this place unfriendly again.

KO: This place has never been friendly: a suspect and a policeman in an interrogation room? No friendship can exist there.

AW Any moment from now, it is you and the torture chamber.

KO: And one has to win.

AW: No one wins the torture chamber.

KO: The torture chamber cannot withstand the firmness of justice!

AW: What justice are you shouting? You kidnapped men who were going about ...!

KO: I did not kidnap those men!

AW: Then who did?

KO: You should know. I should ask you.

AW: It is you and your group who go about kidnapping people!

KO: And the police should know who and who is

responsible for every kidnapping.

AW: The police are no magicians!

KO: Maybe not.

AW: Yes, they are not. They do their best to help the nation maintain law and order!

KO: That is not all we need. The people are still hungry!

AW: I know, but that should not encourage lawlessness!

KO: It is not lawless to fight for a right!

AW: It is not! But when such a fight transforms into destructive tendencies ...

KO: Nothing is destructive in our fight!

AW: Everything about your fight is destructive! You go about blowing up oil pipes, kidnapping people, disrupting the peace ...!

KO: There was never peace ...!

AW: You don't understand that what you are doing is destroying your own properties and that of future generations!

KO: We have never been made to feel we own those things.

AW: Yes it belongs to you, to me, to all of us! We must conceive a new vision that will make us live amicably as a nation.

KO: That is what I want, too. What we all wanted

until the locusts came to raid our harvests. Now we demand …

AW: There is no more demand. It is the vision which must start working.

KO: What vision?

AW: The vision for a new nation where our wealth will be used for the common good of all. A nation where our land will no longer be plundered and depleted, where our voices will find the right tune in the ears of our leaders, where we shall hold our hands and call one another "brothers".

KO: Brothers?

AW: Brothers – Yes, brothers; that word must come back to find its meaning within us.

KO: With all the pains of the past?

AW: That should not deter us. You yourself said maybe tomorrow it will heal. Those pains will end up as forgotten memories. We will come to live together as one. The North shall find its home in the East. The South shall make kinsmen from the West. That is the vision for our new nation.

KO: You're lighting up the fire in me. That is the vision we've always shared.

AW: We can still live that vision in our lifetime.

KO: Yes, you are right; with friendship and brotherliness.

AW: Trust and unity. But first we have to finish our

business here.

KO: What business again?

AW: Come on, Ken, we are here for something important.

KO: *(Sighs.)* But … but …

AW: There is no "but", for now we must double up because of time.

KO: I thought we talked about vision just now?

AW: Yes, but this is duty.

KO: What about all our talks about friendship and brotherhood just now?

AW: Those talks shouldn't come in the line of duty.

KO: I suspect. I should have known.

AW: So, where are they?

KO: Who?

AW: The men.

KO: Which men?

AW: The men we are looking for.

KO: How am I supposed to know the men you are looking for?

AW: (*Frustrated.)* Kenule!

KO: Yes, Brother.

AW: Don't call me "brother" until you cooperate with me!

KO: (*Chuckles.*) Is that the end of "friendship" and "brotherhood", and our "vision"?

AW: Kenule, stop getting on my nerves!

KO: Calm down, Friend.

AW: Where are they?

KO: I don't know.

AW: You know! You know!

KO: I don't know!

AW: (*Advancing menacingly to him, rolling up the sleeves of his shirt.*) You know! And you're going to tell me now!

KO: (*Withdrawing.*) I don't know a thing!

AW: Talk now!

KO: There is nothing to talk! (*Knocks coming from the door.*)

AW: Speak up, Man! Speak!

KO: The door! Someone is at the door!

AW: Leave the door alone and face your business!

KO: Brother, you won't harm your kinsman in this senseless interrogation.

AW: You said ... oh! Those three words; "brother", "kinsman", and "senseless", those words will not make me furious like you, but they will not get in the line of my duty. (*Knocks continue on the door.*)

KO: The door!

AW: I said leave the door alone! And who the hell is at the door! (*The two policemen creep in.*)

POLICEMEN: (*Timidly.*) Information, Sir!

Signal, Sir!

Direct, Sir!

And from headquarters, Sir!

At 5.25 pm direct, Sir!

And 5.28 pm headquarters, Sir!

AW: Will you shut up and speak one by one!

POLICEMEN: Yes, Sir!

At 5.25 pm, Sir!

A call direct, Sir!

And at 5.27 pm, Sir!

A signal from headquarters, Sir!

As an emergency, Sir!

AW: Say what you want to say and stop this ... this absurd acting!

POLICEMEN: Information, Sir!

And signal at the same time, Sir!

At 5.25 pm, Sir!

And 5.27 pm, Sir!

AW: (*Frustrated.*) Alright give the information and scram out of here both of you!

POLICEMEN: The phone ring at 5.25 pm, Sir!

And the radio roger at 5.27 pm, Sir!

AW: (*Perplexed.*) The information straight!

POLICEMEN: That is where we are going, Sir!

And we don nearly reach there, Sir!

AW: Alright, give it to me!

POLICEMEN: The two people, Sir!

The foreigners, Sir!

Wey dem kidnap, Sir!

Taking hostage ...

AW: Will you stop frustrating me and tell me what you want to tell me ...!

POLICEMEN: Sorry, Sir!

AW: Sorry for yourselves. So, what happened to them?

POLICEMEN: Who, sir?

AW: The white men!

POLICEMEN: Which white men, Sir?

AW: Oh my God! The men that were kidnapped!

POLICEMEN: Oh, sorry, Sir,

We no know they are white men, Sir!

AW: (*Sighs.*) Holy Moses!

KO: Please, speak up. What is it with them?

POLICEMEN: Dem don see Holy and Moses, Sir!

And discover ...

AW: Who the hell are "Holy" and "Moses"?

POLICEMEN: The white men, Sir!

AW: Are those their names?

POLICEMEN: You said so, Sir!

AW: (*Totally frustrated.*) Somebody, please help me!

POLICEMEN: Oga, no faint, Sir!

Dem don find dem, Sir!

AW: Where?

POLICEMEN: A team of crack team, Sir!

Wey AIG ...!

AW: Where!

POLICEMEN: In Zuhita, Sir!

At about ...!

AW: Spare me the details! Which group is responsible?

POLICEMEN: Na hin we wan tell you, Sir!

The information say that ...!

AW: Which group!

POLICEMEN: The other group, Sir!

Wey come attack police dat day, Sir!

AW: And?

POLICEMEN: "And" no dey there, Sir!

But information say make you free suspect, Sir!

Sake of say, dem don catch dem, Sir!

AW: Catch who?

POLICEMEN: The group wey kidnap dem, Sir!

Including their leader, Sir!

AW: Alright, you can leave.

POLICEMEN: Can we go, Sir?

AW: Go! (*They leave.*) Well, Kenule, I am …

KO: No need for apologies. You are doing your duty. Thank God I am free now. I must tell you that I have learnt so much in this short time with you, but I must ask when I will be allowed to leave here. The fish and beer in Burutu are waiting for me.

AW: You will leave immediately, but I want to remind you not to forget our vision for tomorrow, the vision for a new nation.

KO: I will always remember that and …

AW: We're friends and brothers.

KO: Yes, we're friends and brothers.

AW: I will live to cherish the memories we have shared, and respect our vision for the coming generation.

KO: I will, too. And I want to tell you, that I love you as my brother.

AW: I will keep that in mind forever. I will also like to advise you to think seriously about your group. Think about turning it into a more promising group for the betterment of our nation.

KO: I am already thinking about that. I may even need to leave the town for a while, to a place where I will be able to rest and think of a better way to contribute to the development of my country.

AW: That is the spirit! Maybe it will take a while before we see again. Anywhere you are, just let our song continue to echo that vision we both share for this country.

KO: Which of our songs?

AW: Our "Che". Che Che kule!

KO: Yes! Che Che kule!

(*They both sing and do the war dances more vigorously than the earlier one. The two* POLICEMEN *stealthily peep to savour the display.*)

AW: My brother, if you wish, you may leave now. All you need to do is just to sign some documents, collect your things and pay some money.

KO: Money?

AW: Oh yes, I forgot. The bail. You will need to pay some stipulated amount for the bail.

KO: But ... bail? I have been released.

AW: Yes, bail. You have been released on bail.

KO: (*Pointing to the "BAIL IS FREE" poster on the wall.*)

But then, bail is supposed to be …

AW: *(Smiles.)* Oh that? It is a mere decoration for now. We don't live it. It is the procedure here that you must pay. If you will come to my office, I will tell you some things that you don't understand. Some things you may never understand, things that even I don't understand in this office. That is why we must watch the situation before we strike.

KO: Just like Ehud!

AW: Yes, just like Ehud in the Bible! Just a little patience, a little plan and maybe tomorrow, tomorrow that we both dreamed of, maybe we'll start to live by those things.

KO: Yes, my brother. Maybe tomorrow … maybe.

(Both exit with KENULE *at the rear. His hands clasped together at his back while he stares and nods continually at the "BAIL IS FREE" poster on the wall. Soft music begins in the background. Light gradually dims.)*

END.

Kraftgriots

Also in the series (DRAMA) *(continued)*

Emmanuel Emasealu: *The Gardeners* (2008)
Emmanuel Emasealu (ed.) *The CRAB Plays I* (2008)
Emmanuel Emasealu (ed.) *The CRAB Plays II* (2008)
Richard Ovuorho: *Reaping the Whirlwind* (2008)
Sam Ukala: *Two plays* (2008)
Ahmed Yerima: *Akuabata* (2008)
Ahmed Yerima: *Tuti* (2008)
Niyi Adebanjo: *Two Plays: A Market of Betrayals & A Monologue on the Dunghill* (2008)
Chris Anyokwu: *Homecoming* (2008)
Ahmed Yerima: *Mojagbe* (2009)
Ahmed Yerima: *The Ife Quartet* (2009)
'Muyiwa Ojo: *Memoirs of a Lunatic* (2009)
John Iwuh: *Spellbound* (2009)
Osita C. Ezenwanebe: *Dawn of Full Moon* (2009)
Ahmed Yerima: *Dami's Cross & Atika's Well* (2009)
Osita C. Ezenwanebe: *Giddy Festival* (2009)
Peter Omoko: *Battles of Pleasure* (2009)
Ahmed Yerima: *Little Drops ...* (2009)
Arnold Udoka: *Long Walk to a Dream* (2009), winner, 2010 ANA/NDDC J.P. Clark drama prize
Arnold Udoka: *Inyene: A Dance Drama* (2009)
Chris Anyokwu: *Termites* (2010)
Julie Okoh: *A Haunting Past* (2010)
Arnold Udoka: *Mbarra: A Dance Drama* (2010)
Chukwuma Anyanwu: *Another Weekend, Gone!* (2010)
Oluseyi Adigun: *Omo Humuani: Abubaka Olusola Saraki, Royal Knight of Kwara* (2010)
Eni Jologho Umuko: *The Scent of Crude Oil* (2010)
Olu Obafemi: *Ogidi Mandate* (2010), winner, 2011 ANA/NDDC J.P. Clark drama prize
Ahmed Yerima: *Ajagunmale* (2010)
Ben Binebai: *Drums of the Delta* (2010)
'Diran Ademiju-Bepo: *Rape of the Last Sultan* (2010)
Chris Iyimoga: *Son of a Chief* (2010)
Arnold Udoka: *Rainbow Over the Niger & Nigeriana* (2010)
Julie Okoh: *Our Wife Forever* (2010)
Barclays Ayakoroma: *A Matter of Honour* (2010)
Barclays Ayakoroma: *Dance on His Grave* (2010)
Isiaka Aliagan: *Olubu* (2010)
Ahmed Yerima: *Mu'adhin's Call* (2011)
Emmanuel Emasealu: *Nerves* (2011)

Alex Roy-Omoni: *The Ugly Ones* (2011)
Osita Ezenwanebe: *Adaugo (2011)*
Osita Ezenwanebe: *Daring Destiny* (2011)
Ahmed Yerima: *No Pennies for Mama (*2011*)*
Ahmed Yerima: *Mu'adhin's Call (*2011*)*
Barclays Ayakoroma: *A Chance to Survive and Other Plays* (2011)
Barclays Ayakoroma: *Castles in the Air (*2011*)*
Arnold Udoka: *Akon* (2011*)*
Arnold Udoka: *Still Another Night* (2011)
Sunnie Ododo: *Hard Choice* (2011)
Sam Ukala: *Akpakaland and Other Plays* (2011)
Greg Mbajiorgu: *Wake Up Everyone!* (2011)
Ahmed Yerima: *Three Plays* (2011)
Ahmed Yerima: *Igatibi* (2012)
Esanmabeke Opuofeni: *Song of the Gods* (2012)
Karo Okokoh: *Teardrops of the Gods* (2012)
Esanmabeke Opuofeni: *The Burning House* (2012)
Dan Omatsola: *Olukume* (2012)
Alex Roy-Omoni: *Morontonu* (2012)
Dauda Enna: *Banquet of Treachery* (2012)
Chinyere G. Okafor: *New Toyi-Toyi* (2012)
Greg Mbajiorgu: *The Prime Minister's Son* (2012)
Karo Okokoh: *Sunset So Soon* (2012)
Sunnie Ododo: *Two Liberetti: To Return from the Void & Vanishing Vapour* (2012)
Gabriel B. Egbe: *Emani* (2013)
Isiaka Aliagan: *Oba Mama* (2013)
Shehu Sani: *When Clerics Kill* (2013)
Ahmed Yerima: *Tafida & Other Plays* (2013)
Osita Ezenwanebe: *Shadows on Arrival* (2013)
Praise C. Daniel-Inim: *Married But Single and Other plays* (2013)
Bosede Ademilua-Afolayan: *Look Back in Gratitude* (2013)
Greg Mbajiorgu: *Beyond the Golden Prize* (2013)
Ahmed Yerima: *Heart of Stone* (2013)
Julie Umukoro: *Marriage Coup* (2013)
Praise C. Daniel-Inim: *Deacon Dick* (2013)